Waste

Debbie Nevins

MEDIA ENHANCED BOOKS
AV2 BY WEIGL™
ADDED VALUE · AUDIO VISUAL

www.av2books.com

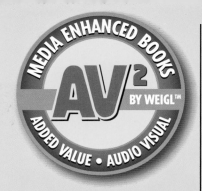

AV² provides enriched content that supplements and complements this book. Weigl's AV² books strive to create inspired learning and engage young minds in a total learning experience.

Go to **www.av2books.com**, and enter this book's unique code.

BOOK CODE

Y679922

AV² by Weigl brings you media enhanced books that support active learning.

Download the AV² catalog at **www.av2books.com/catalog**

Your AV² Media Enhanced books come alive with...

Audio
Listen to sections of the book read aloud.

Video
Watch informative video clips.

Embedded Weblinks
Gain additional information for research.

Try This!
Complete activities and hands-on experiments.

Key Words
Study vocabulary, and complete a matching word activity.

Quizzes
Test your knowledge.

Slide Show
View images and captions, and prepare a presentation.

... and much, much more!

AV² Online Navigation on page 48

Published by AV² by Weigl
350 5ᵗʰ Avenue, 59ᵗʰ Floor
New York, NY 10118

Website: www.av2books.com   www.weigl.com

Library of Congress Control Number: 2013941893
ISBN 978-1-62127-440-7 (hardcover)
ISBN 978-1-62127-446-9 (softcover)
ISBN 978-1-62127-836-8 (single-user eBook)
ISBN 978-1-48961-723-1 (multi-user eBook)

Printed in the United States of America in North Mankato, Minnesota
1 2 3 4 5 6 7 8 9 0 17 16 15 14 13

062013
WEP220513

Weigl acknowledges Getty Images as its primary image supplier for this title.

Every reasonable effort has been made to trace ownership and to obtain permission to reprint copyright material. The publishers would be pleased to have any errors or omissions brought to their attention so that they may be corrected in subsequent printings.

Project Coordinator: Aaron Carr
Art Director: Terry Paulhus

Waste

CONTENTS

Introduction to the Waste Crisis

Waste, or garbage, is piling up around the world. Waste causes many problems. Not only is it unpleasant to look at, but it can also cause serious harm to people and the environment. Current methods of dealing with waste are not perfect. As more and more waste accumulates, the problem of what to do with it grows as well.

The Waste Problem

"Since the **Industrial Revolution**, people have created huge amounts of waste that cannot be recycled."

Types of Waste

"Waste comes in many forms, ranging from household garbage to spent nuclear fuel. Each type presents different problems."

Dealing with Waste

"Industrialized nations produce the most waste but also do a better job of managing it. Waste disposal is a more serious problem in the developing world."

Toward a Sustainable Future

"The answer to solving the waste problem lies in sustainable approaches, such as reducing, repairing, reusing, **recycling**, and renewing."

The Waste Problem

KEY CONCEPTS

1 History of Waste

2 Closed-Loop Systems

3 Disposable Products

4 Garbage at Sea and in Space

5 Environmental Impact

Throughout history, people have created things to make life better. They have created shelter, food, clothing, tools, vehicles, and many other objects. Today, humans produce more things than ever before, but this also creates waste. Manufacturing creates **byproducts**. Merchandise becomes worn out, broken, outdated, or unwanted. What should people do with all their garbage?

1 History of Waste

Most people like to keep waste out of their living areas. To do this, people have developed waste disposal systems. Ancient Greeks and Romans developed dumps outside their cities. People filled garbage dumps with bones, shells, animal skins, and other **debris** from daily life.

In the Middle Ages, however, the usual way to deal with waste was to throw it out the window. Piles of rotting garbage lined the streets and attracted insects and **vermin**. People did not realize that unsanitary conditions caused disease.

In the 1300s, a sickness called the plague, or Black Death, swept across Europe. It killed millions of people. Historians now believe the disease was caused by bites from fleas that were infected. The fleas were carried by rats. At the time, people had no idea what caused the illness or how it spread. It was not until scientists discovered the link between dirt and disease that people began to see the importance of clearing away waste.

Over the years, waste management improved. However, advances in manufacturing led to much more waste. In Europe, when the Industrial Revolution began in the late 1700s, manual labor was replaced with machines. These new practices spread to North America. This meant goods could now be cheaply made in vast quantities in factories. Many products became more affordable. As a result, the volume of waste began to grow enormously.

During the time of the Black Death, people fled crowded cities to try to escape the plague.

2 Closed-Loop Systems

Before the Industrial Revolution, most waste was **biodegradable**. It would decay, or decompose, over time. This waste was mostly made up of organic materials, such as wood, paper, cloth, bones, furs, or leather. Organic materials were once alive. They decay naturally over time. When organic materials decompose, they often release **nutrients** into the soil, which helps plants grow.

For example, a tree grows and is cut down for wood. The wood may be used to build a variety of objects. Over time, though, the wood decays. Nutrients from the decaying wood enter the soil and help new trees to grow. A complete cycle has occurred, ending where it began, with the growth of a tree. Scientists call this type of cycle a closed-loop system. Nature has many closed-loop systems that recycle Earth's organic materials. Another example is the water cycle. Water evaporates into the air and returns to the ground as rain or snow.

Separating food scraps from other household trash is one way to cut down on waste. The food items can be allowed to decay into a type of fertilizer for home gardens.

However, not all garbage is organic. For centuries, humans have been using and producing inorganic, or **inert**, materials. Rocks, sand, clay, and minerals were never alive and will not decay. Metals, concrete, and bricks will not decay, but they can be recycled. For example, many types of metal can be melted down and reused. Concrete and bricks can be crushed into powder and made into a variety of new materials.

A closed-loop system does not produce waste products. Since the Industrial Revolution, however, people have broken the loop. They have created huge amounts of waste that cannot be recycled.

Should People Buy Convenience Food Products?

Consumers are buying more and more products that are packaged for convenience. People can buy precut apple slices wrapped in plastic, grapefruit sections in jars, packaged frozen mango chunks, or canned cherries. Candy, cereal, and all sorts of other food items are available in one-portion, small sizes, which are often packaged inside larger plastic bags or boxes.

These products have a huge impact on the problem of waste. Americans discard 570 million pounds (259 million kilograms) of food packaging every day. Much of this waste could be reduced by buying products with less packaging, such as whole fruits.

Packaged Food Industry
Convenience is an important trend in the food industry. We want to offer many product choices to our customers. Also, we will make more money, which will help the economy.

Consumers
Convenience products often cost more money than other products, but they save us time and effort. We lead busy lives, and these products help us.

Environmentalists
These products are ultimately harmful to the environment. We understand why people want convenience in their active lives. However, the best way to reduce waste is to not create it in the first place.

Activists
Convenience food products often cost much more than basic products. Why should people pay more for packaging? The packaging is just a source of garbage.

| For | Supportive | Undecided | Unsupportive | Against |

3 Disposable Products

In the 20th century, factory-produced goods became plentiful and cheap. This led to a new way of thinking about the objects used in everyday life. Manufacturers once produced products that were meant to last. Now, products were meant to be used for a short time and thrown away.

In 1932, the phrase "planned obsolescence" was introduced. It describes the practice of producing products that are meant to have a short useful life. Such objects wear out, break, or become outdated fairly quickly. Examples of these products include shoes, toys, appliances, and cars. Toward the end of the 20th century, this practice expanded to include electronic devices, such as cell phones and laptop computers.

"Waste from synthetic materials is not biodegradable."

Today, people use and discard objects on a daily basis. People are more wasteful than ever before. In 2010, Americans threw out about 250 million tons (227 million tonnes) of trash.

In addition to inventing new products, people invented new materials, such as plastics. These synthetic materials made waste disposal a much more serious problem. This is because waste from synthetic materials is not biodegradable. Some of it is even harmful to the environment.

One-use products, such as disposable diapers, greatly increase the amount of household waste a family creates.

4 Garbage at Sea and in Space

As trash piles up on land, it also accumulates in oceans, rivers, and lakes. These waters are clogged with marine debris, which is waste found in natural bodies of water. No one is sure how much debris is in the ocean, but the National Oceanographic and Atmospheric Administration (NOAA) is doing research to find out.

Marine debris comes from many sources. Waste washes into oceans from rivers and storm drains, which are the sewers in streets that carry off rainfall. Litter on beaches is carried into the ocean by wind and waves. Companies and individuals dump material into the sea. However, marine waste is hard to measure. Scientists cannot easily see what is on the ocean floor.

In some parts of the ocean, marine debris accumulates in dense patches. The largest of these patches is the Great Pacific Garbage Patch in the northern Pacific Ocean. Scientists estimate that this area of garbage floating between Hawai'i and California is twice as large as the state of Texas. The swirling ocean currents pull floating debris together and prevent it from escaping.

In the Great Pacific Garbage Patch, much of the debris is plastic. It will never disappear. It simply breaks into smaller and smaller pieces. Seabirds and larger marine animals become tangled up in discarded fishing nets and other trash. Smaller **organisms** may choke on tiny bits of plastic.

Even outer space is cluttered with waste, called space debris. Space debris includes parts of launch rockets, disabled spacecraft, dead batteries, dust from rocket motors, and refuse from human missions. Today, there are some 22,000 artificial items about the size of a softball orbiting Earth. There are more than 135 million pieces that are even smaller. All of this space waste could damage spacecraft or satellites.

Entanglement in marine debris kills thousands of seabirds, fish, sea turtles, and marine mammals each year.

5 Environmental Impact

Garbage is spoiling Earth in many ways. Litter is not only ugly, but it can also be hazardous to wildlife. Garbage dumps, or landfills, may leak toxic, or poisonous, chemicals into the surrounding soil and **groundwater**. This can contaminate the environment. Burning trash can send toxic gases into the atmosphere, polluting the air.

Industrial processes also affect the environment. People are not always aware of industrial and agricultural waste. However, **sewage**, **sludge**, construction debris, and polluted water make up a great deal of the waste problem facing the world. This waste cannot be easily reused, so it must be disposed of.

Waste is a problem on a global scale. In **developed countries**, waste management has improved in recent decades. Laws have caused industry to act in a more responsible way.

However, **developing countries** often do not have such protections. People in these countries often do not have sanitary facilities, so they dispose of garbage in any way they can. They throw garbage into the rivers, burn it openly, or discard it in unregulated dumps that attract vermin and flies. In addition, some developed countries have made matters worse by exporting their hazardous waste to developing nations. This has caused severe environmental damage.

Natural places damaged by waste are costly to clean up.

Should the United States Ban Excessive Packaging?

In the United States, packaging materials make up as much as 44 percent of **municipal solid waste**. Almost every kind of product sold, including toys, food, and electronics, is often packaged in many layers of plastic, styrofoam, and cardboard. Packaging materials clog landfills. These materials are often made of products that are not biodegradable.

Statistics show that, in the United States, 1 million plastic shopping bags are used every minute, and about 16,000 are distributed daily. Although a plastic bag takes only a second to manufacture, it requires 100 to 400 years to degrade. In 2003, Great Britain passed a law prohibiting manufacturers and retailers from using excess packaging. Should the United States do the same?

Concerned Consumers
Yes. We are tired of over-packaged products, which are very hard to open. We are also concerned about the environment. Excessive packaging is not necessary.

Retailers
Some of us are responding to customer concerns about excessive packaging. Some online retailers now offer consumers a choice about how products are packaged.

Store Owners
Packaging helps improve our sales by making products look attractive on the shelf. Also, packaging for small items helps prevent shoplifting.

Manufacturers
Packaging performs many tasks. Certain kinds of packaging keep products clean and safe from damage during shipping. Clear plastic lets consumers see the product before buying it.

 For   Supportive   Undecided   Unsupportive   Against

Types of Waste

KEY CONCEPTS

1 Municipal Solid Waste

2 Wastewater

3 Industrial, Agricultural, and Construction Waste

4 Hazardous Waste

5 Nuclear Waste

Waste comes in many forms, ranging from household garbage to spent nuclear fuel. This is fuel from nuclear power plants that can no longer be used. Each type of waste presents different problems. Some kinds carry germs or unpleasant odors. Others pose extremely serious threats to humans and animals.

1 Municipal Solid Waste

The municipal solid waste (MSW) that people throw out every day includes biodegradable items, such as food scraps, newspapers, and grass clippings. It also includes items such as plastic bottles, metal pots and pans, and appliances. Mixed in are some things that may contain toxic substances. These include old batteries, medicines, and electronics.

MSW is typically picked up by garbage collectors and hauled to landfills. The Environmental Protection Agency (EPA) reports that, on average, every person in the United States throws out about 4.5 pounds (2 kg) of trash per day. Not all of it ends up in a landfill. Some is recycled or **composted**. In 2010, about 136 million tons (123 million tonnes) of MSW were discarded in U.S. landfills.

In 1980, the amount of solid waste Americans generated was lower than it is today. The figure was about 3.7 pounds (1.7 kg) per person per day. By 2010, MSW per person had increased by 20 percent.

Household waste from private homes and apartment buildings makes up about 55 to 65 percent of the total MSW in the United States. The rest of the waste comes from commercial and institutional locations, including businesses, schools, and hospitals.

What Do Americans Throw Out?

Many different materials make up municipal solid waste in the United States.

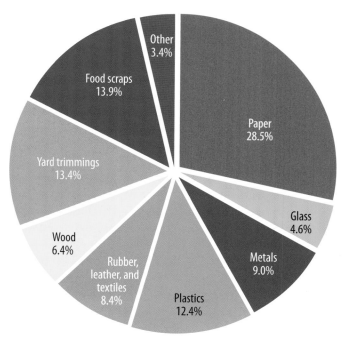

Other 3.4%
Food scraps 13.9%
Paper 28.5%
Yard trimmings 13.4%
Glass 4.6%
Wood 6.4%
Rubber, leather, and textiles 8.4%
Metals 9.0%
Plastics 12.4%

Percentages are for the year 2010.

2 Wastewater

Wastewater consists of the things that get flushed down the toilet or go down the drain. In homes, that includes human waste and water used for washing dishes, cleaning laundry, and taking baths and showers. It also includes chemicals from household cleaners.

Industrial wastewater is more complex. Depending on the industry, this water can include a number of chemicals, metals, and organic compounds. Agricultural and food industry wastewater can contain insecticides, animal wastes, body fluids from animals, hormones, antibiotics, and more.

Wastewater is treated, or cleaned, at sewage treatment plants. There, the waste materials are removed from the water. They are concentrated into a muddy deposit called sludge. The treated water is released into nearby rivers and oceans.

Years ago, sludge was often piled onto barges, shipped offshore, and dumped into the ocean. In the United States, the Ocean Dumping Ban of 1988 prohibited this practice, beginning in 1992. However, some other countries still dump sludge. Today in the United States, sludge is buried in landfills. Some of it is turned into a kind of compost, which is used on agricultural land.

For centuries, most sewage was left untreated. It was simply piped to the nearest body of water. Today, large amounts of untreated sewage still flow into rivers and oceans worldwide, polluting coastal waters and damaging marine life. This practice is more common in developing countries.

About 90 percent of the wastewater produced globally is left untreated.

Should There Be Tougher Laws on Lawn Care?

Homeowners and gardeners in charge of parks, golf courses, and local government properties must work to keep lawns free of weeds. A perfect lawn often requires pesticides to kill insects and herbicides to kill weeds. These substances may contain toxic chemicals. These chemicals can rub off on people and animals. They can also contaminate groundwater. Certain pesticides used in the United States have been banned in other countries.

A safer, more natural approach to lawn care is possible. Some people even think that lawns should use native plants instead of grass. That way, chemical treatments might not be needed.

Environmentalists
Yes, laws would be a good idea. Many pesticides have not been adequately tested. Many are linked to serious health problems. There are safe, natural ways to keep lawns healthy.

Families
Chemicals used on lawns are especially dangerous for animals and children. We worry about exposing our kids and pets to danger on our lawns and in local parks.

Local Governments
We would like to use an all-natural approach to treating the grass in parks, schoolyards, and government properties, but it is too expensive. We cannot afford the additional labor and materials.

Lawn Care Industry
People want beautiful lawns. Our products are registered with the EPA and are not considered hazardous. When used according to the directions, lawn care products do not represent a significant threat to people or pets.

For	Supportive	Undecided	Unsupportive	Against

3 Industrial, Agricultural, and Construction Waste

Manufacturing, agriculture, construction, and mining produce most of the world's waste. Metal works, chemical plants, paper-making factories, food-processing plants, and many other types of manufacturing operations produce many kinds of toxic waste. Countries in the developed world produce millions of tons (tonnes) of this waste each year.

Agricultural waste includes manure, which is animal dung used to fertilize farmland. Agricultural waste also includes materials that remain after crops are harvested, such as stalks, stems, and roots. In many cases, this waste can simply be plowed back into the soil. Large farms, however, can produce so much waste that it cannot be recycled or reused.

Waste related to construction includes building materials and debris from demolishing, or tearing down, buildings. The weight and variety of construction waste often makes it difficult to dispose of or recycle.

Mining activities create the largest amounts of solid waste. After mining, excavation materials, such as dirt and rocks, are left over. This waste is often dumped close to mine sites. In some countries, mining companies are now required to clean up their waste. Before these laws went into effect, mining companies did not have to follow such rules. Heaps of ugly, sometimes toxic, waste were left behind once mines had closed down.

Some mining operations in developing countries continue to pollute land and water. For example, a gold and copper mine in Irian Jaya, Indonesia, generates hundreds of thousands of tons (tonnes) of waste each day. This waste contaminates nearby rivers and the Indonesian rainforest, threatening the health and safety of plants and animals.

At some old factory sites, containers of toxic materials sit and corrode for years after the business has closed.

4 Hazardous Waste

Waste is considered hazardous to people or the environment if it is toxic, explosive, destructive, or capable of causing fire or infection. Thousands of harmful substances are in use around the world, and many more are created every year. Traces of these substances travel long distances through air and water. They can cause damage everywhere from the Arctic to the Amazon rainforest.

Today, electronic devices quickly become outdated as newer models of cell phones and computers become available to the public. Unwanted electronics are called e-waste. In the United States, alone, about 150 million old cell phones were discarded in 2010. Between 2006 and 2010, Americans threw away 1.24 million tons (1.12 million tonnes) of computers.

Old computers and monitors are often made of plastics and other synthetic materials. They contain substances called **heavy metals**, which can cause pollution and are often toxic. Examples of these substances are lead and mercury. These metals are especially toxic to children and pregnant women.

Some hazardous wastes break down, but some can remain toxic for years. These hazardous wastes are known as persistent organic pollutants (POPs). Not only do most POPs disrupt **ecosystems**, but they are also very dangerous to animal and human health.

In the United States, laws now require any hazardous waste spill to be reported to government officials and cleaned up immediately.

5 Nuclear Waste

In 2013, there were more than 400 nuclear power plants throughout the world. Of those, about 100 were in the United States. Nuclear power plants use the heat from nuclear reactions to generate electricity. The nuclear industry produces less than one percent of the world's waste. That small amount of waste, however, causes a great deal of concern. This is because some of it is **radioactive**.

Radioactive substances are extremely dangerous to human health, emitting tiny particles that can damage living cells. Nuclear waste can include used fuel and materials that have come in contact with radioactive items. Some kinds of radioactive nuclear waste can remain dangerous for thousands of years. To dispose of nuclear waste, it must first be cooled for about 50 years. Then, it can be transferred to a storage facility deep underground. Once there, the material must be kept away from the environment for about 10,000 years.

Today, the issue of what to do with radioactive waste is an important problem. There are 70,000 tons (63,500 tonnes) of **high-level waste** in temporary storage in the United States.

By the 2030s, the United States is expected to have more than 90,000 tons (82,000 tonnes) of spent fuel. Stocks of this waste also continue to pile up around the world. Scientists and governments are looking for a permanent solution.

Another problem with nuclear waste is the possible danger of an accident at a nuclear facility. In 1986, a nuclear accident took place at Chernobyl, Ukraine. More recently, in March 2011, an earthquake off the coast of Japan caused a major **tsunami**. A huge, powerful ocean wave came onshore and damaged the Fukushima Daiichi Nuclear Power Plant, resulting in the **meltdown** of three reactors. A large amount of radioactive material was released into the environment.

Nuclear power provides about 16 percent of the world's electricity.

Should Nuclear Waste Be Sent into Space?

In 2010, President Barack Obama created a commission to determine how the United States should handle its nuclear waste. The final report, issued in 2012, recommended building a permanent storage facility deep underground. People were opposed to a similar proposal to bury the waste at a site in Nevada. That plan was dropped in 2010.

Some people think the best solution is to send nuclear waste into space. Under one such plan, spacecraft carrying radioactive waste would be sent out of the solar system. Other plans are to send the waste straight into the Sun or into orbit around the Sun.

Space Futurists
Sending nuclear waste into space may be expensive and possibly dangerous. However, scientists are working on ways to accomplish this. Once the waste is sent deep into space, it would no longer pose a problem.

Scientists
Some of us feel that disposing of nuclear waste in space is a better option than burying it underground. Launches must be safe, but we can develop the technology need to accomplish this.

Nuclear Industry
We have looked at the idea of disposing nuclear waste in space since the 1970s. We decided that there are too many problems. It would be very expensive, and an accident during launch could release radiation.

Antinuclear Groups
There are enormous costs and risks associated with disposing of nuclear waste in space. There will never be a truly safe way to deal with nuclear waste. We should stop using nuclear energy.

 For   Supportive   Undecided   Unsupportive   Against

Dealing with Waste

KEY CONCEPTS

1 Landfills

2 The Superfund Program

3 Incineration

4 Harmful Emissions

5 Developing Nations

There are three main ways to get rid of waste. It can be dumped and buried. It can be incinerated, or burned. It can also be recycled.

1 Landfills

Dumping has always been the most popular method of waste disposal. Until the 1970s, most landfills were rough, poorly covered garbage dumps. Once they were full or no longer being used, they were simply covered over with dirt. That practice changed, however, when scientists discovered that old landfills could leach, or leak, harmful chemicals many years after they had been buried.

Today, many laws in the United States and Europe guide the construction, operation, and closure of landfills. They are built in places where any leaching will do the least harm. They have special liners to protect groundwater, as well as collection systems to remove **leachate** from any leaking materials. Workers frequently cover the landfill waste with soil to help reduce odors, rodents, and insects.

Some landfills are also designed to make use of energy from gases that are created when certain materials in the landfill decomposes. Methane is one such gas. In addition, fertilizer can sometimes be made from substances in landfills. Landfills are the most widely used method of waste disposal in the United States. The nation has more than 1,800 landfill sites, most of which are located far from populated areas.

A Modern Landfill

Today's landfills have many features designed to keep the environment safe.

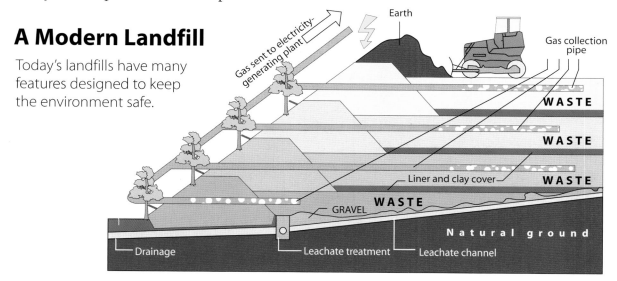

Mapping the World's Waste

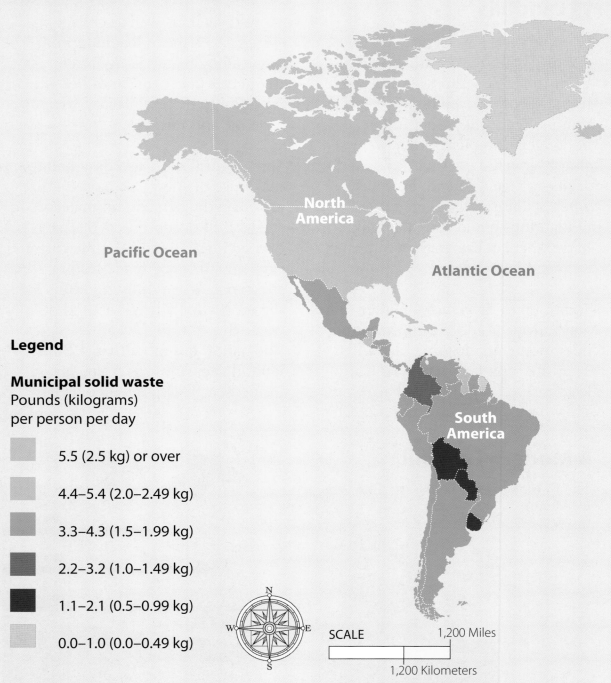

North America

Pacific Ocean

Atlantic Ocean

South America

Legend

Municipal solid waste
Pounds (kilograms)
per person per day

5.5 (2.5 kg) or over

4.4–5.4 (2.0–2.49 kg)

3.3–4.3 (1.5–1.99 kg)

2.2–3.2 (1.0–1.49 kg)

1.1–2.1 (0.5–0.99 kg)

0.0–1.0 (0.0–0.49 kg)

SCALE

1,200 Miles

1,200 Kilometers

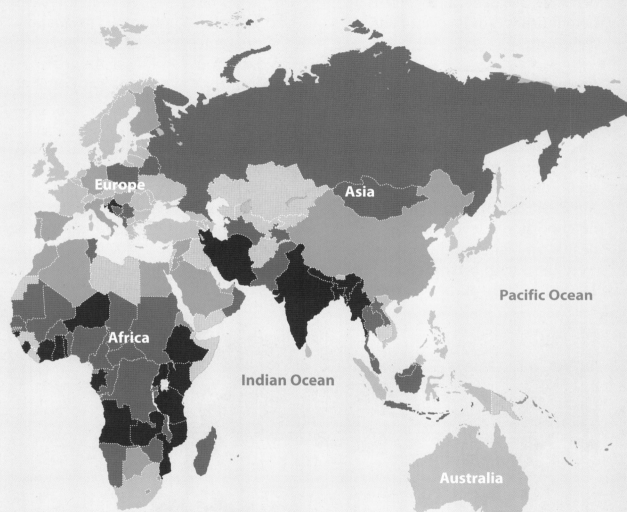

Arctic Ocean

Europe

Asia

Africa

Pacific Ocean

Indian Ocean

Australia

Southern Ocean

Municipal Solid Waste (MSW) by Country

This map shows that the United States and Australia are among the countries whose people generate the most municipal solid waste. On the other hand, people in some African and Asian nations generate very low amounts of MSW. Greenland also generates very little MSW, but it has a very small population.

2 The Superfund Program

Old garbage dumps, which predate modern safety standards, can cause great damage to the environment. One of the best-known incidents occurred at Love Canal. This is a neighborhood in Niagara Falls, New York.

In the 1950s, new homes and a school were built on the site of an old industrial landfill at Love Canal. Over time, toxic chemicals and gases seeped into the groundwater and bubbled out of the ground. Many of the children living in the neighborhood developed severe health problems, and many babies were born with **birth defects**. In 1978, President Jimmy Carter declared a federal emergency in the area. Eventually, the government bought hundreds of homes at Love Canal, and the residents moved away.

In 1980, the U.S. government created the Superfund program. The goal of the program was to identify and clean up dangerous landfills throughout the country. Love Canal was the first site on the Superfund list.

The Superfund program is still going on. The EPA identifies groups that are responsible for contaminated sites and directs them to clean up the sites. Sometimes, the EPA handles the clean-up itself. By 2012, the EPA had more than 1,300 hazardous waste sites on its National Priorities List.

Cleaning up contaminated sites is a complicated undertaking requiring specially trained workers.

3 Incineration

Incineration, which is also known as combustion, presents a possible solution to waste management. Burning quickly eliminates ugly piles of garbage. However, incineration can also pollute the air with toxic **emissions** from the material that is burned.

Years ago, incinerators were very basic. They simply burned up the trash. At that time, people gave little thought to the hazardous emissions being released during burning. They also did not worry about the amount of energy lost in the incineration process.

By contrast, today's incinerating plants in developed countries are built with a range of devices to prevent air pollution. In addition, they are often designed to recover energy. These plants may generate electricity, provide hot water for heating systems, or process heat for manufacturing. Burning waste for energy is becoming more and more popular in many parts of the world. It is especially suited to places that do not have a great deal of open space for landfills. Japan, for example, incinerates up to 80 percent of its municipal solid waste. The United States burns only about 10 percent of its waste. In Europe, the use of incineration ranges widely. Denmark and Sweden incinerate about 50 percent of their MSW. Other countries, such as Greece, do not incinerate at all.

Waste Disposal in the United States, 1960–2009

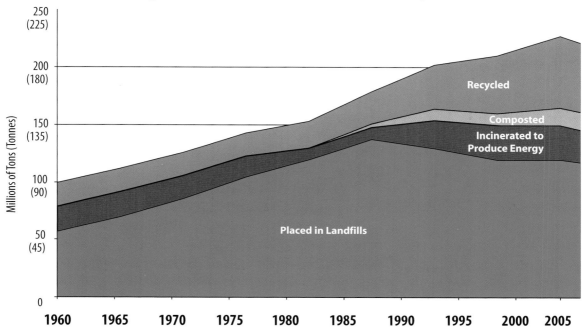

4 Harmful Emissions

Both landfills and incinerators can release harmful gases into the atmosphere. In developed countries, modern facilities greatly reduce that problem. Worldwide, however, many places have serious air pollution problems.

In Beijing, China, for example, harmful emissions from vehicles and industry have made the air quality so poor that many people wear surgical masks when they are outdoors. Sometimes, children are not allowed outside to play. Levels of deadly pollutants in the air can be up to 40 times higher than the levels that the World Health Organization says are safe.

In landfills, when organic matter rots, methane and carbon dioxide are released. These are both powerful greenhouse gases. In the atmosphere, these gases sit like a sheet of glass above Earth, trapping the Sun's heat and making the air warmer than usual. This increase in temperature is known as the greenhouse effect. According to scientists, because of modern industry and other human activities, there are more and more greenhouses gases in the atmosphere. This has helped to cause global warming. Scientists say that as the planet warms, ice caps at Earth's poles may melt, oceans may rise, and weather patterns may change. Some landfills have systems to capture methane and burn it for energy. This prevents the methane from entering the atmosphere.

Modern incinerators include sophisticated systems for removing harmful materials. They scrub away acidic gases such as sulfur dioxide and hydrogen chloride. Incinerator smokestacks are built tall so that gases are widely spread out. However, the wind can carry those gases several miles away from the plant. Therefore, people living close to an incinerator may be affected less than people living **downwind**.

Some people object to the visual pollution, or unsightly appearance, created by incinerator smokestacks.

Is Incineration a Wise Solution to Waste Disposal?

Burning quickly eliminates huge amounts of municipal waste, and incinerators have long been considered a necessary part of waste disposal. Incineration, however, is controversial. Some people do not want incineration plants in their communities.

On the other hand, many incineration plants now convert waste into energy. In addition, a relatively new combustion technology called **gasification** is cleaner than regular incineration.

Crowded Countries
Yes. We do not have enough room for landfills. New incinerators that use gasification and convert waste into energy are safe and efficient. They convert the byproducts of combustion into fuels, chemicals, and fertilizers.

Large Cities
We have nowhere to put our waste. We must transport it over a long distance to get rid of it, using huge garbage trucks. It makes more economic sense to use incinerators that can convert waste into energy than to use landfills.

People Living Near Incinerators
Incinerators, with their tall smokestacks, ruin the landscape. They also may release dangerous substances that are a threat to our health.

Advocates for No Emissions
Rather than treating emissions, we should have no emissions at all. Incineration can make people think the waste problem has been solved. A better solution is to change wasteful lifestyles and unwise industrial practices.

For   Supportive   Undecided   Unsupportive   Against

5 Developing Nations

Developed nations such as the United States produce the most waste. They also, however, tend to do a better job of managing it. Waste disposal is a more serious problem in the developing world, and the problem is getting worse.

Some countries, such as China and India, are rapidly becoming more industrial. They are building roads, digging mines, constructing buildings, modernizing their agriculture, and manufacturing more consumer goods. As they do all these things, these countries are producing vastly greater amounts of waste.

In developing and very poor nations, well managed, sanitary landfills are rare. For example, in Manila, the capital of the Philippines, a large part of the city's daily waste output is dumped outside of controlled landfills. The open heaps of garbage cause health dangers to the surrounding population. Also, poor people often search through these dumps for food, clothing, or other items that they can use or sell. In some places, small children work in the dumps and are exposed to dirt and contamination.

On an even more basic level, more than one-third of the world's population does not have adequate sanitation facilities. These 2.5 billion people do not have toilets, sewers, and wastewater treatment plants. In many cases, they have no sanitary means of dealing with human waste at all. The waste contaminates the soil and waterways of their communities. Such conditions spread disease and cause high rates of **child mortality**.

Children picking through dumps risk being cut by sharp metal, broken glass, or wire.

Should Nations Export Hazardous Waste?

A few decades ago, it was common for industrialized nations to ship their hazardous waste to developing nations, with or without official permission. The developing countries often did not handle that waste safely, which was dangerous to their environment and people.

The Basel Convention, a treaty adopted in 1989, requires countries exporting waste to get permission from the countries receiving the waste. Some people would like to completely forbid the export of hazardous waste to developing countries.

Industrialized Nations
We cannot afford the enormous costs of managing our own hazardous wastes. Our people want to get rid of this waste. Sending it abroad makes better economic sense for us than trying to deal with it at home.

Developing Nations
We need the money that we receive when we take in this waste. It is our decision, and other countries should not tell us what we can and cannot trade. Also, we can sometimes use the waste as a source of metals that we can obtain through recycling.

Environmentalists
The waste that is dumped in developing countries is extremely dangerous to people and the environment. This must be stopped. Industrialized countries must take responsibility for their own waste and stop harming others.

Anti-Export Activists
Pollution is not something to be bought and sold. Rather, it is something to be eliminated. Exporting hazardous waste is like forcing people to trade their poverty for poison.

| For | Supportive | Undecided | Unsupportive | Against |

Toward a Sustainable Future

It may seem as if people are doomed to drown in their garbage, but there are some solutions. The answers may lie in **sustainable** approaches. These include reusing, recycling, and renewing.

1 Reusing and Recycling

Recycling may be one of the best ways to manage a variety of wastes. Already, a great deal of everyday garbage is recycled into useful goods. Paper and cardboard are processed into roof shingles. Metal cans are melted down and made into wire mesh. Colored glass is used in making fiberglass insulation. Newspapers can have the ink removed. Then, the paper can be turned into pulp, which can be turned into newsprint again.

A discarded glass bottle takes about one million years to decompose, but glass is one of the easiest materials to recycle. Some bottles can simply be washed and reused, which saves 80 to 90 percent of the material and energy used to make new bottles. Old glass can also be ground up to form **cullet**, which can then be used to make new glass products.

Recycling is something everyone can do. In 2011, Americans recycled some 61 billion cans. Aluminum cans are the most recycled beverage containers in the world, with a 65 percent recycle rate. It takes 95 percent less energy to recycle a can than it does to make a new one.

2 Renewable Resources

Many of Earth's resources are renewable, which means they will never run out. Examples of renewable resources include solar, wind, **hydroelectric**, and **geothermal** power. The challenge in turning to these resources is that society heavily depends on nonrenewable resources, such as petroleum, coal, and natural gas. Much of today's technology is designed to work with nonrenewable energy. Changing to renewable sources will be expensive and will take time, but advocates argue the advantages will outweigh the costs in the long run.

Even renewable resources, such as water, have to be used with care. A century ago, cities dumped raw sewage into rivers and lakes. This turned clean water into wastewater.

Biomass is another important source of renewable energy. The waste products from agriculture or forestry can be burned to produce electricity. Crops can be turned into fuel, such as ethanol, which is made from corn. Some cars run on ethanol rather than gasoline. Ethanol is a renewable fuel, since new corn crops can be grown.

3 Zero Emissions

Today, many companies have made it their goal to achieve total productivity. This means that they aim to produce no waste, no defects, and no pollution. This is known as zero waste, or zero emissions. It means that instead of traditional waste management, they are looking toward resource management.

People have come to use the word "waste" to describe not only garbage but also the inefficient use of resources. For example, about 90 percent of the energy in a car's fuel is lost in wasted engine and exhaust heat. Only 10 percent is used to power the vehicle. The auto industry is gradually changing to address that concern. In the future, more vehicles will feature lightweight bodies, high fuel efficiency, and no polluting emissions.

Many other industries are also looking at ways to reduce the wastefulness of their activities. If consumers support companies that use environmentally responsible production methods, then industries will be motivated to make changes.

Ranking Waste Management Methods

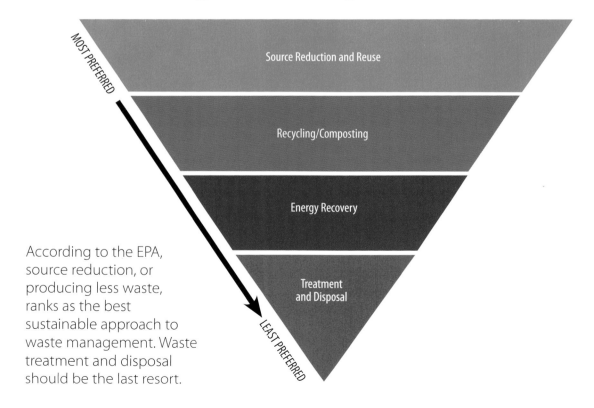

MOST PREFERRED

Source Reduction and Reuse

Recycling/Composting

Energy Recovery

Treatment and Disposal

LEAST PREFERRED

According to the EPA, source reduction, or producing less waste, ranks as the best sustainable approach to waste management. Waste treatment and disposal should be the last resort.

Is "Zero Waste" a Realistic Goal?

Many communities also require the recycling of paper, plastic, and glass. Recently, some groups, such as the Zero Waste Alliance, have been supporting the idea of "zero waste." They say that recycling is not enough.

The goal is a complete elimination of waste. That includes zero emissions, including greenhouse gases, as well as zero landfill waste and zero water waste. Several large corporations have announced zero waste as a business goal. Meanwhile, some individuals and families are attempting to live a zero-waste lifestyle.

Activists

Zero waste is an important goal for a sustainable future. It can be achieved through the work of everyone in our communities, including businesses, industries, schools, and homes. Waste should be thought of as a potentially usable resource.

Proponents of Recycling

Zero waste is a really just a working principle. We can create less waste, but we probably cannot totally eliminate it. The point is to start planning for the elimination of waste rather than managing waste.

Doubters

Most people and industries are not interested in zero waste. They talk about it to make it seem as if they are making a difference. The truth is that humans will always produce garbage. We simply have to figure out how to manage it better.

Incineration Industries

Zero waste is unrealistic, and it will probably not occur anytime soon. Recycling is good, but it has problems, too. The modern incineration industry has facilities that can turn waste into energy. This is more realistic.

For   Supportive   Undecided   Unsupportive   Against

Waste through History

The history of waste and waste management is part of the history of human civilization. Communities have always faced challenges maintaining their quality of life while handling their waste. As people learned more about the effects of garbage, they tried to find better methods of waste disposal.

Around 500 BC

Greek and Roman civilizations develop advanced techniques of waste management, including elaborate sewage systems to remove wastewater. In Athens, Greece, a law is passed that requires waste to be disposed of at least 1 mile (1.6 kilometers) from the city.

Around 500 BC

AD 1348–1350

A plague called the Black Death sweeps through Europe, killing one-third of the population. The disease spreads partly because of the poor sanitation and filthy living conditions that are common at the time, due to a lack of waste management.

1885

The United States Army builds the first garbage incinerator in the country on Governors Island in New York City. The same year, the first municipal incinerator opens in Allegheny, Pennsylvania.

1944

The Dow Chemical Company invents the material Styrofoam, or polystyrene. The U.S. government later determines that manufacturing polystyrene produces hazardous waste.

1948

Fresh Kills Landfill opens on Staten Island in New York City. It will become the world's biggest landfill, covering 2,200 acres (890 hectares) and taking in 13,000 tons (12,000 tonnes) of municipal waste every day by the 1990s.

1948

1961

Procter & Gamble introduces Pampers. By 2006, disposable diapers will make up 2.1 percent of municipal waste in the United States.

1970

The first Earth Day is celebrated on April 22, marking what many people consider the beginning of the modern environmental movement. The Environmental Protection Agency is established, and the Clean Air Act is signed into law. The act bans open burning at landfills in the United States.

1972

The Clean Water Act becomes law in the United States.

1976

The Resource Conservation and Recovery Act is passed in the United States, requiring all garbage dumps to be replaced by "sanitary landfills."

1990

McDonald's announces that it will stop using polystyrene food containers due to concerns that this type of packaging stays in the environment for hundreds of years.

2001–2002

Debris from the 9/11 attack on New York City is taken to Fresh Kills Landfill. The landfill is then closed. Preparation begins to transform it into a park. The process is expected to take 30 years.

2011

2011

On March 11, a tsunami hits northeastern Japan. It causes a meltdown at the Fukushima nuclear power plant. Some 5 million tons (4.5 million tonnes) of debris is washed into the Pacific Ocean and is expected to wash up on shore in the United States and elsewhere for years to come.

2012

McDonald's begins to phase out polystyrene coffee cups.

1970

Working in Waste Management

RECYCLING COORDINATOR

Duties Preparing educational programs, arranging for the collection of recyclables, evaluating facilities involved in recycling

Education A bachelor's degree in science

Interest Protecting the environment

Recycling coordinators make sure a community's recycling programs run smoothly and efficiently. They manage the facilities and schedule pickups and deliveries. They also keep track of data, such as contamination levels, recycling rates, and collection amounts. They seek out new ways for the materials to be reused and new ways to sort materials. The job usually involves a variety of work in the office and out in the field.

Recycling coordinators are active within the community. Communication is an important skill for them. They help teach people about recycling and reducing waste, and they sponsor waste collection drives.

HAZARDOUS WASTE MANAGER

Duties Developing and overseeing hazardous waste programs

Education A bachelor's or master's degree in chemistry, biology, geology, or environmental science

Interest Chemistry, math, protecting the environment

Hazardous waste managers work in one of the most dangerous and important fields of waste management. They must deal with toxic chemicals, nuclear byproducts, and organic garbage. Hazardous waste managers are responsible for making sure that safety equipment is in good working order and that chemicals, explosives, or other dangerous materials are properly secured. Hazardous waste professionals develop plans for cleaning up environmental accidents. They also design safe waste-handling systems.

ENVIRONMENTAL SOIL SCIENTIST

Duties Studying and evaluating contaminants in the soil, groundwater, and surface water

Education A bachelor's degree in science and often a master's degree in agriculture

Interest Nature and the outdoors, protecting the environment

Soil scientists are active in a wide variety of fields, including agriculture and landscape design. In waste management, soil scientists are concerned with the quality of soil and water. They might investigate how a hazardous waste facility or a manufacturing plant may be contaminating the ground. They also play an important role in forest management, water quality protection, and land use planning.

Soil scientists often work out in the field and should enjoy being outdoors. They may need to hike over rough and uneven land to gather soil samples or examine pollution sites.

WASTEWATER PLANT TECHNICIAN

Duties Operating equipment for sewage treatment, sludge processing, and disposal

Education An apprenticeship within the trade

Interest Operating machinery, science, math, clean water issues

Wastewater plant technicians contribute to a cleaner environment by overseeing the processing of contaminated water. They work at sewage treatment plants, monitoring machinery to make sure it is functioning safely and cleanly. Responsibilities include starting and stopping pumps, engines, and generators; taking water samples; and cleaning tanks, filters, and tools. Technicians also maintain a log of operations by recording meter and gauge readings.

Key Waste Management Organizations

EPA

Goal Protecting human health and the environment

Reach National

Facts Employs about 17,000 full-time workers

The United States Environmental Protection Agency (EPA) was established by President Richard Nixon in 1970. As an agency of the federal government, it is committed to keeping the nation's environment safe. It works to set policy, establish national standards, and enforce environmental laws.

The EPA's priorities include taking action on climate change, improving air quality, protecting the nation's waters, assuring the safety of chemicals in manufactured products, and cleaning up communities.

UNEP

Goal To provide global leadership and encourage partnership in caring for the environment

Reach Worldwide

Facts Launched the Global Partnership on Waste Management in 2010

The United Nations Environment Programme (UNEP) coordinates the environmental activities of the UN. It arose after the UN sponsored a Conference on the Human Environment in 1972 to discuss global pollution problems. UNEP is an international organization that has its headquarters in Nairobi, Kenya. It has six regional offices located on different continents. UNEP evaluates environmental conditions around the world and educates the global community. It also works to create international agreements that support wise environmental management.

GREENPEACE

Goal Defending the natural world and promoting peace by investigating, exposing, and confronting environmental abuse, and championing environmentally responsible solutions

Reach Worldwide

Facts The largest independent direct-action environmental organization in the world

Greenpeace, founded in 1971, is a broad-based environmental organization committed to nonviolent activism. It is interested in all issues relating to environmental safety, including global warming and the destruction of forests. Problems relating to waste, such as hazardous waste production, e-waste, chemical waste, and nuclear waste, are also great concerns for Greenpeace.

NRC

Goal Supporting waste reduction and sound management practices for raw materials in order to realize an environmentally sustainable economy

Reach North America

Facts Has more than 6,000 members

The National Recycling Coalition (NRC) supports and promotes the recycling industry. It is a nonprofit group that helps its members to convince community leaders, decision makers, and the news media that waste reduction, reuse, recycling, and composting lead to more jobs and a healthy economy. Members include people working in all areas of waste management, such as local recycling coordinators, state and federal regulators, corporate environmental managers, environmental educators, consumers, and waste management professionals.

Research a Waste Management Issue

The Issue

Waste is a subject of much debate. Many groups may not agree on the best way to decrease the amount of waste or how to dispose of it. It is important to enter into a discussion to hear all the points of view before making decisions. Discussing issues will ensure that the actions taken are beneficial for all involved.

Get the Facts

Choose an issue (Political, Cultural, Economic, or Ecological) from this book. Then, pick one of the four points of view presented in the issue spectrum. Using the book and research in the library or the Internet, find out more about the people or groups that support your chosen point of view. What is important to them? Why are they backing or opposing the particular issue? What claims or facts can they use to support their point of view? Be sure to write clear and concise supporting arguments for your group. Focus on the environment and how the group's needs relate to it. Will this group be affected in a positive or negative way by changes in the environment around them?

Use the Concept Web

A concept web is a useful research tool. Read the information and review the structure in the concept web on the next page. Use the relationships between concepts to help you understand your group's point of view.

Organize Your Research

Sort your information into organized points. Make sure your research clearly answers what impact the issue will have on your chosen group, how that impact will affect it, and why it has chosen its specific point of view.

WASTE CONCEPT WEB

Use this concept web to understand the network of factors affecting waste management.

- Increased production leads to increased waste
- Increase in disposable products
- Nonbiodegradable or toxic materials
- Excessive packaging

- Improperly managed waste attracts vermin, spreads disease
- Air, soil, and water pollution
- Marine debris impacts ocean life
- Nonbiodegradable, hazardous, and nuclear waste build up in environment

- Pollution affects entire Earth
- Emerging nations often have substandard waste management practices
- Global economies must support best practices in waste management

Consumer Culture

Global Issue

Environmental Problems

Waste

Sustainable Future

Disposal Options

Regulations and Oversight

- Recycling and composting can be done on an individual basis
- Zero emissions goal
- Zero waste lifestyle, with the goals to reduce, reuse, and recycle

- Modern landfills prevent seepage, cause release of greenhouse gases
- New incinerators reduce harmful emissions
- Landfill and incineration can produce energy

- Government agencies, such as the EPA, have the ability to enforce laws to protect health and safety
- Independent organizations impact public opinion and help produce solutions

Test Your Knowledge

Answer each of the questions below to test your knowledge of the waste issue.

1 What is a closed-loop system?

2 What does the term biodegradable mean?

3 What is the term for the everyday trash from homes and businesses?

4 What is the most common form of waste disposal in the United States?

5 What activity creates the largest amount of solid waste?

6 What is e-waste?

7 Why is nuclear waste a major safety concern?

8 What is the Superfund program?

9 Approximately what proportion of the world's population lacks adequate sanitation facilities?

10 Give four examples of renewable energy resources.

7

8

6

5

U.S. EPA SUPERFUND PROJECT

BLUFF ROAD SITE

NO TRESPASSING

FOR FURTHER INFORMATION
CALL
MICHELLE GLENN
(404) 347-7791

10

Key Words

biodegradable: capable of being broken down into harmless products through the action of living things, such as microorganisms

biomass: plant materials and animal waste that are often used as a source for fuel

birth defects: problems or abnormalities that are present at birth

byproducts: items produced when another substance is made

child mortality: the rate of deaths among children

composted: organic matter that decays into plant fertilizer

cullet: broken or waste glass used to speed up the melting process in the manufacture of new glass

debris: garbage or waste

developed countries: countries with high average income and advanced technology

developing countries: countries with low average income that until recently had little manufacturing and technology

downwind: in the direction in which the wind is blowing

ecosystems: communities of plants and animals interacting with their environment

emissions: gases or other substances released into the air

gasification: a method of incineration that changes municipal solid waste into a synthetic gas

geothermal: energy produced from Earth's interior heat

groundwater: water below the surface that supplies wells and springs

heavy metals: certain metals, such as mercury, plutonium, and lead, that can be harmful to people and the environment

high-level waste: a type of nuclear waste created by the reprocessing of spent nuclear fuel

hydroelectric: electricity generated by converting the energy of flowing water

Industrial Revolution: the rapid development of industry, beginning in the 1700s in Great Britain, brought about by the introduction of power-driven machinery

inert: not capable of decaying

leachate: the liquid produced in a landfill from the decomposition of waste

meltdown: in a nuclear reactor, the overheating and melting of fuel elements in the core

municipal solid waste: the mix of toxic and nontoxic garbage generated by households and businesses

nutrients: things needed by people, plants, and animals to live and grow

organisms: forms of life

radioactive: emitting charged particles as a result of the breaking up of atoms

recycling: converting waste into usable material

sewage: water that goes down the drain or is flushed down the toilet

sludge: a soft, thick, muddy substance produced in sewage treatment processes

sustainable: capable of being maintained without harming the environment

tsunami: a very large ocean wave caused by an underwater earthquake or volcanic eruption

vermin: small animals or insects that carry disease, such as rats and cockroaches

Index

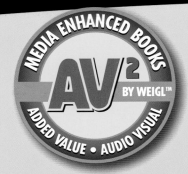

Log on to www.av2books.com

AV² by Weigl brings you media enhanced books that support active learning. Go to www.av2books.com, and enter the special code found on page 2 of this book. You will gain access to enriched and enhanced content that supplements and complements this book. Content includes video, audio, weblinks, quizzes, a slide show, and activities.

AV² Online Navigation

Audio
Listen to sections of the book read aloud.

Book Pages
AV² pages directly correspond to pages in the book.

Video
Watch informative video clips.

Key Words
Study vocabulary, and complete a matching word activity.

Embedded Weblinks
Gain additional information for research.

Quizzes
Test your knowledge.

Slide Show
View images and captions, and prepare a presentation.

Try This!
Complete activities and hands-on experiments.

AV² was built to bridge the gap between print and digital. We encourage you to tell us what you like and what you want to see in the future.

Sign up to be an AV² Ambassador at www.av2books.com/ambassador.